SCOUTING BY NIGHT

SCOUTING BY NIGHT

Being a sequel to
"THE VALUE OF OBSERVATION IN WAR."

BY

FREDK. G. COOKE

Assoc.M.Inst.C.E., M.S A.,
EASTBOURNE VOLUNTEER TRAINING CORPS.

FULLY ILLUSTRATED
with Diagrams and Photographs

The Naval & Military Press Ltd

Published by

The Naval & Military Press Ltd
Unit 5 Riverside, Brambleside
Bellbrook Industrial Estate
Uckfield, East Sussex
TN22 1QQ England

Tel: +44 (0)1825 749494

www.naval-military-press.com
www.nmarchive.com

In reprinting in facsimile from the original, any imperfections are inevitably reproduced and the quality may fall short of modern type and cartographic standards.

CONTENTS.

	PAGE
Preliminary Remarks...	1
A Scout's Equipment	7
Close Study of your Surroundings by Day Necessary for Night Work	11
Scouting by Night	16
Sounds by Night	18
Scouting by Night between the Trenches and in the Open ...	28
Scouting in and about Farm Buildings	39
Going by the Stars	44
Use of Luminous Compass	48
Concluding Remarks	58

Photographs by G. & R. Lavis, Eastbourne.

SCOUTING BY NIGHT.

Considering that about half our lives are spent in darkness, and that so much fighting is done at night, it is time we were all educated to deal with its trials and difficulties, just as blind men are to cope with their grievous disability.

The average man is rather a weak creature in the dark, especially in the open country. He is, then, a little lower than the animals; even sheep have some discretion at night, but their lambs are not "lullabied" to sleep by terrifying bogey and ghost stories. Nurses (their name is legion) who thus fill children with a frenzied fear of darkness are doing very wicked work, in that they are weakening the fibre of the rising generation.

Unfortunately literature, ancient and modern, teems with references to darkness as a fearful thing.

Some poets are great sinners in this respect. One defines night as "the mother of human fear." This is quite cheering! Another, referring to night, tells of—

> "The sullen sigh the prowling panther heaves,
> Save the fierce growling of the cubless bear,
> Or the tramp of gaunt wolf rushing from its lair
> Where its slow coil the poisonous serpent weaves."

Quite good this: just right for the nursery! But some of us would like to hear the "tramp" of a wolf. What a pity this poet didn't dilate on the terrific clamour of an owl's wings!

Now I will tell you what a man amongst men had to say about darkness.

David was a subtle Scout; he, during many months, successfully eluded King

Saul's patrols, who tried by dark and by day to catch him in the Wilderness, and failed. What does he say in the Psalms of darkness, he who knew it so well?

"THOU SHALT NOT BE AFRAID FOR THE TERROR BY NIGHT."

This is a message worthy of a great soldier. Let us all act up to it by treating even Egyptian darkness as a mere sporting difficulty to be overcome.

After all, night is "black, but comely," once you master it; all fear falls from you then, only the wonder and the witchery remain.

Only those who toil, shoot, fish, or fight at night realise its variety and marvellous charm. The moon, for instance, is never so bright as when it lights "your necessary path," the stars never so brilliant as when they point the way, deep shadow never so welcome and profound as when it shrouds you from the foe, and helps you unseen to see or to slay, without being slain—the first duty of a soldier.

But night is a wayward mistress; she now and again slily lures the wildfowler into far away marshes by the Will o' the Wisp of apparently perfect weather, and anon buffets him back against raging wind and blinding snow and rain, bedraggled and done. Yet a Scout must sometimes wait for and encounter the very weather a wildfowler avoids and dreads; he will need all his night-craft then. There is ever so much to learn, and little time to do it in, before he goes to the Front.

My own most exciting experience of intense darkness was in surveying the course of a curved tunnel deep underground. On reaching the end, which was blind, the light went out, owing to excess of carbonic acid gas. There was some peril; the bottom of the tunnel was very rough, water was heavily spouting out, above and below; a fall would have been serious owing to the foul gas on the floor of the tunnel. I realised then the meaning of the words "blackness of darkness." Getting back was a little trying, but a mere trifle compared with the dangers encountered daily by our soldiers at the Front in driving tunnels towards the enemy trenches.

There is amusement, as well as ordeal, in the dark. Once, when wildfowling late on a moonlight night, after a heavy snowfall, with a long white nightdress over my clothes, and wearing a white cap (a Scout at the Front in snowy weather would naturally act somewhat similarly), I shot a duck, and accidentally splashed myself with blood. While passing a hillock I came suddenly across a belated farm labourer.

Practically all he could see on the snow was a gun and a dark splash. He was very startled. I slipped away silently, and possibly he thought he had seen a ghost.

Naturally a Scout, like the owl, the fox, and all predatory night prowlers, should be properly equipped so, as far as possible, to be neither seen nor heard, winter and summer alike. The Service uniform is unsuited for scouting; however, it is easily covered. A Scout then won't look much like a soldier perhaps, neither did David when, clad as a shepherd boy, he slew Goliath. "Shining armour" went down miserably before observation and instant initiative in a smock frock. Uniforms don't make trained soldiers.

Diagram No. 1 shows the nature of the work a Scout may have to do between the trenches, such as reporting on enemy working parties, new trenches, detecting mining, cutting barbed wire, locating snipers and dealing with them, leading bombing parties, engaging patrols, and so on.

For hazardous enterprises like these a Scout should be highly trained at home now, and most certainly he should have proper equipment: it is cheap enough. A clever Scout is worth his weight in gold.

A Scout's Equipment.

There should be no exposed buttons anywhere on a Scout's coat to catch up or click when creeping. The knees of the knickers should be very strong, possibly leather-lined externally, then soft stuff could be inserted to protect his knees, or, better still, special pads, similar to those shown on Diagram No. 2.

A Scout must at all times have means ready to instantly cover his hob-nailed

DIAGRAM No. 1.

of Operations
ark night
)ecting
 Snipers, Listening Posts,
, also Mining, Sapping
renching

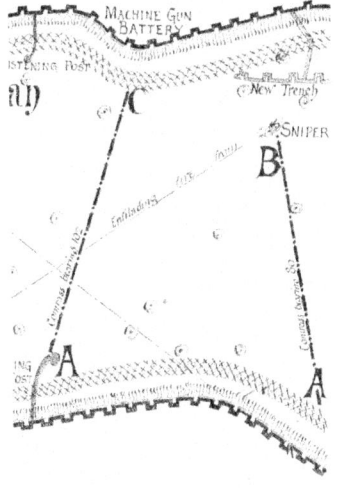

s from A A A to Machine
t B, Working Party at D,
ck at E.

DIAGRAM No. 2.

Sketch showing Scout's knee pads alternatively available as pads for boots.

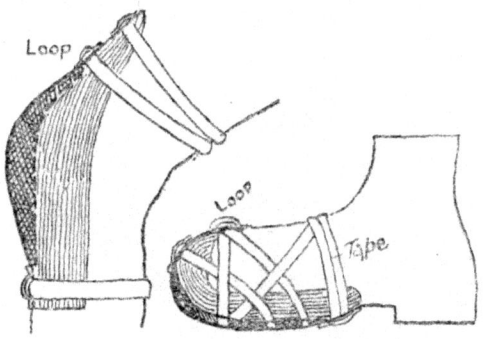

Same pad on sole to deaden sound like a moccasin.

Pocket filled with 8 yards of strong tape, muslin face covering, or any soft useful material.

REGD. 651547

PHOTOGRAPH No. 3.

Scout using knee pads alternatively as moccasins on his boots, rapidly and silently crossing gritty ground.

Scouting. *To face Page 9.*

boots and toe-caps so that he can get across hard, gritty ground silently (see Photograph No. 3). The knee pad can alternatively be used for this purpose. Elbow joints should be padded; he can then lever himself along quite comfortably when going on his stomach over rough ground.

When ground is hard frozen and little snow then the going is very bad and noisy, as I know only too well.

Muslin, coloured in summer, white in winter, round head and neck when there is snow will tend towards invisibility on moonlight nights. I spent some days on snow shoes in a Russian forest in midwinter clad in a white sweater, white cap, gloves, and white thigh boots—a very suitable equipment for snow weather in the trenches.

Thick mitten gloves, with the buttons on

top of the wrists, will prevent injury from stones, glass, thorns, bits of barbed wire, fragments of shells, etc., when you creep, and creep you must very often.

As for arms, personally I should prefer a revolver on very dark nights—better a short carbine than a rifle.

A combination chisel in a sheath is desirable; one you can kill with or prize open doors, cut openings in brickwork or fences, climb trees with, dig holes. If made with a suitable socket, it can be fixed to a stout loaded stick, and used like a lance; no mean weapon in the dark. You can carry a chisel in your puttees.

A clasp knife with a saw edge on a long blade is very handy; you can silently saw any thick branches in getting through hedges, etc., or cut down barbed wire posts. A wire-cutter of the latest pattern must be carried.

A luminous watch and compass are requisite, also binoculars.

A longish length of stout webbing will enable a Scout to improvise many things. String, of course, and a length of supple copper wire will be useful.

On special occasions carry a bomb or two.

In studying your equipment remember that silence is never so golden as at night.

Put duplicate brace buttons on your trousers.

CLOSE STUDY OF YOUR SURROUNDINGS BY DAY NECESSARY FOR NIGHT WORK.
(See Page 53.)

Wellington's faculty of locality was profound; he could almost invariably tell the nature of a country unknown to him far out of sight by a close study of what he could see. No mere guess work this, but just deductive observation in its highest sense, showing the supreme importance of always studying your country surroundings in a military sense wherever you go at home or abroad, and you are hardly a soldier unless you do.

To begin with, select a fairly easy open district, and get to know it, not casually or lazily from a motor car or motor cycle, but by sturdily walking over it, always alone, not necessarily with a map—these are useless at night. The only way is to sketch important features on the spot, and sometimes from memory at home, as a check. You will not easily forget what you have laboriously put on cardboard, even if you do so scores of times. I can personally answer for that. Take compass bearings frequently (don't be offended if I poke a little fun at some of you), and then on a moderately dark night take a bee line, say, from Concert Coppice, avoiding Cinema Bog, to Duty Hill. Another night go from Promenade Pond, past Theatre Wood, crossing Love Lane, skirting Band Hollow, to Efficiency Farm; you will get plenty of true soldierly entertainment in so doing, and the intense satisfaction of feeling you are training your ears, eyes, and feet in night work, ready for the time to come when you are at the Front. It will be awkward then for those whose knowledge of the "country" is mainly confined to pavements; there will be vain regrets then, perhaps more than that. It's bad to be wounded or killed uselessly, but it must be a very awful thing to blunder and let your pals in wholesale, which you may do if you are not good at getting about at night.

The following extract from "The Times," 27th August, 1915, tells of a mistake in the dark—in consequence, many brave men died, and a great opportunity was lost.

THE NIGHT MARCH FROM ANZAC, DARDANELLES.

"Everything depended upon our surprising the enemy. Unfortunately our guides had taken the wrong path! The night was very dark, and sometimes it was difficult to distinguish the forms of our men."

However, the enemy makes mistakes too —more disastrous still. According to "The Times," 13th September, 1915, a German correspondent states that the British landing in Suvla Bay was a complete surprise. The Turks' watching was bad. He goes on mournfully to say "that if there had only been a single German on watch that night the British Army, 40,000 strong, would never have landed."

Here is a pen picture of a nervous sentry, "Morning Post," 9th August, 1915 :—

"Then came the nervy one, and our peace of mind departed. First it was Germans, and I got my bombs ready; then it was gas, and I got my smoke helmet out; then he saw a rabbit, and I called him rude names, etc., etc."

All the training in the world would not make a Scout of this particular "soldier."

The instances quoted above prove that the value of an army can only be measured by the all-round efficiency of each individual soldier. A single alert Turk could have easily prevented, or hindered at fearful cost, our landing in Suvla Bay that memorable night in August last.

An army composed entirely of clever Scouts would be almost as terrible as the Britons who fought from Mons to the Marne, the most magnificently trained soldiers the world has ever seen. You are soon to join " all that is left of them." It is up to you to equal their unbroken endurance, their overmastering skill. It was these powers that prevailed, not simply courage—which is common enough. Only perfect training will enable a soldier to cope with all occasions, especially at night.

Scouting by Night.

Now let me tell you how to rob the blackest night of some of its terrors and difficulties.

In the day time your horizon may be bounded only by miles, at night by the fraction of a yard sometimes. In short, you are wholly blind, but your sense of touch, hearing, and smell is thereby rendered intensely acute. However, to gain the immeasurable advantage of that acuteness, you must first eliminate fear. Once that is accomplished you can with pure enjoyment develop all your powers of touch, hearing, and smell to the highest pitch. You will then be no longer really blind, nor need you be in the least degree nervous.

Very specially remember that if you are blind so must your foes be. All are equal in that respect in the dark. Realise this to the full, and you will soon lose any sense of fear.

Do not strain your eyes when sight is difficult or impossible, concentrate all your powers on listening intently, but it is very little good to listen vaguely. A Scout should first consider what sounds he is likely to hear, and from previous study should be able to know what particular noises may portend.

Sounds by Night.

Unset sounds, like jewels in the rough, are difficult to determine if you are inexpert.

The costliest gems are the tiniest, the most ominous sounds may be mere murmurs; they usually are. For instance, the faint tremor which tells of mining.

Most noises presaging danger at night are man-made. You should define, separate, and concentrate on particular ones (previously studied) out of a confusing medley of other sounds; it can be done. It is a well-known fact that finely trained musicians can separate and enjoy the strains of a 'cello, for instance, in an orchestra of many instruments, practically excluding all other sounds. Anyone can hear the ringing defiant blast of a bugle call clearly above almost any tumult, so by training you will be able to detach much less strident sounds, and after a little practice very faint ones.

My own hearing is highly trained to detect the plop of rising trout out of "the sound of many waters," also the gentle "phee, phee, phee" of wild ducks' wings, betwixt and between other sounds, when flight shooting, even on rough nights; also the lap of water against boats and the sound of rowlocks and oars. Not one man in a score would succeed in so doing, but no man can accurately tell whence these sounds come; that is the greatest difficulty of all. Dogs can tell, and instantly face the right direction, pointing their ears thereto; birds at rest do the same. Our ears are set sideways, partly forward, not behind. A hare's ears, on the contrary, are set for pursuing sounds (a wise provision of Nature) therefore turn your head so that one ear fronts the suspected direction, concentrating your whole attention on the expected sound, judiciously ignoring all others.

To catch sounds immediately behind turn your head over your shoulder, keep otherwise quite steady. Study laboriously and classify, when alone, different sounds, such as those made by men walking, running, crawling, and creeping on hard and soft ground, through long grass, **tall crops, undergrowth,** on ground strewn with leaves and twigs, in water, on planks, and in all ways.

The sound of men mustering "en masse" or marching.

You ought to know French and German words of command, and certainly swear words; English ones may be familiar.

Historians state that "the English swore horribly in Flanders." Doubtless the Germans also swear; they have reason to, sometimes.

Next you must listen for, and try to discern, hard breathing, sniffing, and coughing, and also the following sounds.

Noises made in trench digging by spades and pickaxes; these will differ according to the geological formation; study this point.

Driving tunnels. In this (though you may hear without it) you want the assistance of a special tube, which, when inserted in the earth, will enable you to detect sounds, and accurately locate the tunnel.

When listening for tunnelling without a tube extend the fingers of both hands into the earth, or insert a stick in the ground, and put the other end against the outside of your ears or your temple. Always put the stick on a stone below the surface, it collects vibrations. Sounds will reach your ears through your skull. You will find this useful on very rough nights full of conflicting sounds, and rough nights are best for scouting sometimes.

The thud of crowbars punching holes, hammers on posts, usually padded to deaden the sound, the fixing of planks, mixing concrete, cutting wires, repairing roads, and work generally.

The thud of horses' hoofs, all paces, especially over wood bridges.

The click of breech blocks and metal generally.

Push bicycles on all sorts of ground.

Wheel traffic of all sorts.

The hum of aircraft.

The dip of oars, the noise of rowlocks in boats; the approach of shipping.

The cries of birds when alarmed, and the swish of their wings. Rats abound at the Front, study their little ways; they usually squeal when in company.

If you study all these sounds you will be able to recognise them; each differs from the other.

When in a listening post you should classify and ignore sounds made by your comrades behind you.

High wind makes many noises; branches of trees may creak and groan; it will even lash pond-water into waves so that you can hear them; odd things about you will rustle alarmingly sometimes, making sounds you wouldn't even notice in day time.

Gun and shell explosions, far and near, will distract your hearing at times. This applies equally to the foe; never forget that. Your ears will suffer less when a shell bursts near you if you keep your mouth open, so don't clench your teeth.

In cutting barbed wire, do it as quietly

as possible. Wire stretched taut will spring back noisily, unless you are careful.

When you hear suspicious sounds keep perfectly still; wait till you gather what's afoot before you act. Don't crouch in a cramped attitude, but in an easy position, so that you can turn or strike in any direction without losing your balance. Be very careful how your feet are placed, especially on muddy or slippery ground. A golfer takes infinite pains over his stance, so does a flight shooter; he needs to, for his chance of shooting is momentary, so may yours be.

Be sure your hear perfectly, and that you have nothing on that creaks, such as leather braces, leggings, or boots.

You will hear sounds on soft ground best if you put one ear parallel with it and close to it. Try also with your face forward.

Hold your head up for all other sounds, especially distant ones.

The surface of still water, and wood, both conduct sound to a very special extent. Beware of any road or path made up on wood.

In foggy weather, sounds are heard more plainly; the patter of rain deadens it, so a rainy night is a good one for operations. Sounds are heard more clearly down wind.

If you are listening under a wall for sounds the other side of it put your ears over the top, or at an opening, if it is safe to do so, or as near the top as you can.

If when scouting you can put a wall, a building, high banks or bushes between yourself and your objective you will be less easily heard.

Sound echoes and reverberates in streets and between high walls, increasing the noise of footfalls, especially over roads and pavements. Even the soft plump of a policeman's indiarubber soles is very noticeable if he uses his feet badly.

Sound travels at the rate of 380 yards a second, under 5 seconds a mile, and quicker in summer than winter. The higher the altitude the less quickly sound travels. Pockets in the air, especially in valleys, hinder sound. Sound travels through metal ten times quicker than through space.

Study night sounds at home; there is much to learn. Go frequently into a lonely rough field, a wood, or along a road with a keen comrade, and practise approaching each other in various ways and at different distances, both up and down wind. It is a very fascinating occupation.

It is fairly easy to approach in almost perfect silence on soft ground, provided you feel with your advancing foot that there is nothing crackly underneath, such as twigs, leaves, branches, stones, gritty places, fir cones, straw, or odd things. If necessary, feel with your foot, three or four different spots first, ever so gently, before you tread firmly.

The faintest click of equipment, creak of a boot, or crack of loose joint, can be detected yards away on a still night.

Take full advantage of any neighbouring noises, which may partially drown yours.

All the time you will be studying other sounds, especially those already mentioned.

Some sounds such as those, for instance, made by men approaching stealthily can only be heard when quite close; this is why it is so important to study such sounds and to know them intimately beforehand.

You can hear a careless footfall on a hard road hundreds of yards away on a still night. It is, however, very difficult to tell how far off sounds are, also if approaching or retiring, say, a patrol, for instance, or a body of men. Still it is only a matter of practice, combined with thoughtful concentrated listening.

Suppress somehow or other any tendency to exclaim "Oh!" or anything aloud when you unexpectedly fall or hurt yourself badly; however you may smart, be as silent as a shadow.

Kipling's description of a destroyer,
　　"200 feet of shod death,"
is perfect.

Work hard and become
　　"Six feet of sure silent death,"
then you will be a Scout.

SCOUTING BY NIGHT BETWEEN THE TRENCHES AND IN THE OPEN.

Don't go over dangerous ground until you have been away from artificial light

PHOTOGRAPH No 4.

Scout feeling his way with a stick on a black dark night is saved from a bad fall.

Scouting. *To face Page 29.*

for a good half hour or more, and so got night eyes.

If desirable, move forward or retire quickly the moment a flare has gone out—those observing will have temporarily lost their night eyes.

Never go out on a scouting expedition when it is really dark, or over very rough unstudied ground, without a long pointed stick, such as Australian black trackers use. A Zulu stabbing assegai would be doubly handy, but the end of your stick must not have a metal spike; it would click on hard ground, and spoil the sense of touch up to your hand. I have dealt fully with the advantages gained by using a stick in my first lecture, "The Value of Observation in War." Use your stick as an elephant does its trunk: in front, around, behind, and above, and as silently (see Photograph No. 4). A loop of cord attached to the top of the stick will enable you to use both hands and still retain the stick.

If it is moonlight, take advantage of all shadows, watch any clouds; wait, if necessary, till the moon is obscured; even low ridges and undulations cast shadows. Remember that if the moon is behind you your shadow will precede you. This applies equally to flares, especially when rearward, even at a considerable distance.

Flares immediately above may be less perilous.

Veterans know exactly the noise of explosions causing a flare to ascend, and either get into the nearest hole or instantly freeze themselves to the ground, remaining absolutely still till the light has gone out and the rifle or machine gun fire ceased.

If when scouting alone, or in company, you come into close quarters, for instance, with a hostile patrol, specially remember that neither side can accurately judge the numbers opposing.

Frequently at the Front strong enemy patrols have retreated before one or two dauntless British Scouts. When you are in a tight place, bluff yourself out of it. The enemy dreads cold steel. Sit or lie tight, and keep cool.

On light nights, short cuts along ditches, hedges, or easy ways leading straight to the enemy are dangerous. Always steer a devious course when time and cover admit; there are such things as fixed rifles.

If there is a moon don't forget it or trust too much that clouds will continue to shroud it. A British patrol was recently wiped out because the moon was not considered.

Study wind, weather, and the horizon, changes may be both rapid and inconvenient, especially as it may take you three hours or more to go 100 yards.

Old soldiers will tell you that when fighting is going on along trenches the enemy will hide in holes and "dug-outs" and come out and shoot our men in the back after they have passed. Search all likely hiding places as you go by wherever you go. You may find a hostile sniper, but he may get you first if you are unobservant. A sniper can only get to an isolated position at night, probably before dawn. If you spot his location, deal with him surely, possibly with a deftly flung bomb.

Always look out for, and avoid touching, trip wires, about 9 inches above the ground. They may be connected with flares or alarm contrivances. There may be a machine gun trained along that wire.

When near hostile trenches it will be imperative sometimes to move with extreme deliberation, inch by inch, and remain perhaps for hours even in one place.

"More haste less safety" is a fine motto for Scouts.

Go for practice, preferably on a dark, rainy night, into a field where there is a defined grassy footpath, and try never to lose it; feel carefully with your feet, your stick, and hands too sometimes. If the field is bounded by ditches you will be more careful how you act. Continue practising under varying conditions many times.

It will be necessary very frequently to creep on your stomach; practise doing this constantly, especially retreating feet first; it is an art not easily learnt. A stick will help you to push yourself along, so will a rifle if you know how to use it, but the breech must be covered. However, don't use the butt of a rifle on hard ground. You will probably wish to return exactly as you came: that is a little difficult sometimes.

If you are reconnoitring a trench a hundred yards away or so on a very black night you can leave a trail, paper chase fashion, at intervals, or leave a track by means of string, luminous or otherwise, by which you can make signals by code, and return to the exact spot you started from, but there are obvious objections to this unless it is artfully done.

Before you set out note which way the wind blows; it will help you to know your way back and to interpret sounds which are, of course, more plain down wind.

If there is little wind, and you are doubtful of the direction, wet both cheeks; you will then know which way it is blowing. Your cheeks are far more delicate than your fingers.

Objects not noticeable in the day time may loom surprisingly large at night; then there is practically no perspective, no colour, little detail, no distance, and you cannot see through foliage. A bunch of thistles, for instance, may look quite solid. Specially study this very awkward phase of night work; it is extremely important.

Things you know well in the day time may look totally different at night, particularly when there is fog or haze.

You will sometimes have to make instant and vital decisions, but avoid panic. For instance, you may think you are discovered, as you may be, but coolly and steadily make sure; then act. Go back slowly zig-zag fashion, if time and surroundings admit, facing the foe. He won't be sure you are alone, but most certainly he will hope you will get up and bolt, because you are practically demonstrating that you are alone, then you are probably doomed. However, if there is absolutely no alternative, rush back, turn and twisting like a hare, till you reach cover; then face back again and shoot, or not, as may be, then off again.

Random rifle fire in the dark is seldom effective. Let the enemy blaze away, revealing his position and strength, and then after a long interval you may be able to put in a bomb with effect; no one can tell from what point a bomb comes, but your first duty is to Scout and report. Run no risks—a dead Scout is of no value except to the enemy. If you are really expert, he would lose several of his own men to get you; so disappoint him.

A Scout should travel as light as possible, but on special occasions a couple of sandbags would be convenient; he could fill and decorate them with twigs, and form a screen to retreat to, or to observe from, on open ground; or push a couple on sticks, toboggan fashion, very slowly, inch by inch, in front of him, just as wild-fowlers do (see Photograph No. 5). When there is snow, white linen bags would be

PHOTOGRAPH No. 5.

Scout wearing green hood on his shoulders, green muslin over his face and knee pads, cautiously pushing inch by inch screen of rushes in front of him to disguise its approach over open ground.

Scouting

To face Page 36.

least visible. Some wildfowlers even paint their guns white.

Be careful about cutting wires: you might explode a mine if you interfere injudiciously, or immediately advertise your presence.

A dead horse or cow, minus its interior, may contain a sniper; it has proved so at the Front. Smelly no doubt, but effective.

Faggots of brushwood, gorse, sheaves of corn, rushes, etc., can be made use of. You can fashion these when compulsorily lying up; a length of webbing will aid you. (See Scout's Equipment.)

When walking in the dark lift your feet more than in the day time, you will be less liable to trip, and keep both feet quite parallel; you will hold your balance better, and not present so wide a front to catch obstructions as when you put your toes splayed outwards.

A wise Scout settles on probable lines of retreat as he goes along. Before he sets out from a trench he takes care his comrades know the direction he is taking, but doesn't call out the information. There may be a hostile Scout within easy hearing.

On bright moonlight nights, and at dawn, look up occasionally, especially when in and near woods and buildings; trees and roofs may contain snipers. Look out for tracks and signs generally; you can always tell which way a man has crawled through long grass and tall crops by the direction the disturbed growth takes. Consult your luminous watch occasionally. The light comes suddenly at dawn, which may be awkward.

Specially consider skyline, it is astonishing how a man's shape shows up at night. Observe how plainly cattle, trees, posts, buildings and solid bodies generally can be seen against a night horizon.

Look back constantly night or day, especially with a view to getting back, and keep an eye on the horizon all round.

SCOUTING IN AND ABOUT FARM BUILDINGS.

(See Diagram No. 6.)

There will be no live stock close to the firing line, but a Scout should be ready for all occasions. The unexpected happens sometimes.

About 3.0 a.m. is a good time to scout buildings, for at that hour the vitality of human beings is lowest, and sleep most difficult to resist, but beasts and birds may be very wide awake, especially as they will be hungry. Go up wind if possible. Consider wind even before light.

Two men at least are required to scout extensive buildings, one or more behind in support, but, above all, be sure your companion is staunch, of proved ability, and

Scout's Course in
FARM B

Way shown

Scout keeps to Lee-
ward of DOG,
DUCKS & GEESE
and avoids going
through any
GATEWAY

Direct
shown

DIAGRAM No. 6.

and around typical
JILDINGS

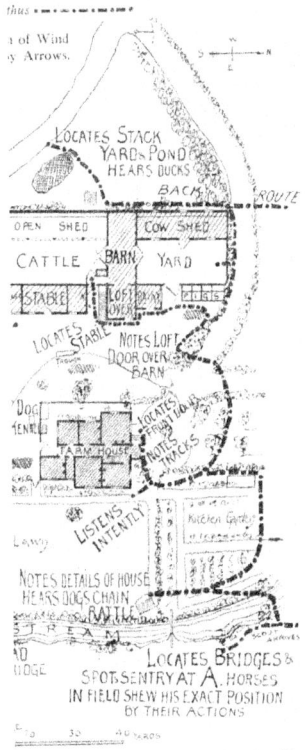

does not cough every few minutes. You must obey orders of course, but in most cases you will achieve more, and run less risk, if you go alone. Then you are responsible only for your own skin, and no need to think of a possibly nervy companion.

In going round any corner, don't at any price let your shadow go first, and as far as possible always look round on your right or firing side. If you are fairly sure there is no one behind you lie down, and look round corners of buildings, walls, and enclosures. Close to the ground your head will be less easily seen, especially on a light night. You may get horribly dirty; that you must put up with (see Photographs 7 and 8). Scout any barn or place where men are likely to sleep; note if doors are open or loopholed; if so, there is probably someone inside. If moonlight, you may see tracks, even on thresholds, also in gate-

PHOTOGRAPH No. 7.

Soldier incautiously looking round brick stack with head and shoulders unnecessarily exposed.

PHOTOGRAPH No. 8.

Scout at full length on ground looking round corner of brick stack.

ways and soft ground. Always get under an open fence or gate rather than over it; make a bit of a hole if necessary. Never go through a gateway or over a bridge if you can avoid doing so. Specially beware of plank bridges, they may be set to catch you, accidentally sometimes, as I once found to my cost.

If your mission is to fire stacks or buildings, take some paraffin; you may not succeed without it, especially on a wet, windy night—a fuse may be necessary. Only little boys and girls invariably succeed in lighting stacks. Consider the wind, also what effect the glare may have on your line of retreat.

Men coming out of a lighted room into the dark cannot see well for some time; it is useful to remember this; you can act accordingly.

Notice nature and position of any ladders, especially near big stacks; also notice the disposition of wagons, rollers and carts, and what they contain.

Look out for loopholes in walls, outside steps and stairs, wells, water tanks, and ponds. Tins and "debris" of all sorts may teach you something in the dark if you use your nose and hands.

Doors to stables, barns, and outhouses usually open outwards. Make a mental note of all such details in case an attack is to be made later; then just previously you might fix doors; from outside arrange to rush wagons against them, or break down walls, fences, and gates; disable ladders or remove them.

Ducks are sometimes used as "watchdogs." The Romans effectively employed geese on a celebrated occasion. Moor hens are very wakeful at night.

There will usually be a dog in the back yard of a farmhouse. Ducks and geese will be housed near a pond close to a stack yard, and even when penned are dangerous. Fowls and chickens in sheds may be ignored. A Scout in training should visit large and small farm steadings, and the live stock therein, and study them by day; he will find his knowledge useful at the Front.

High wind will carve alarming shapes out of herbage, branches, reeds, and odd things which flap, especially round buildings.

In scouting around any range of buildings observe relative positions thereof and important details, such as doorways, especially to stables, gateways, etc., with a special view to being able to make a fairly accurate sketch plan from memory on your return. It is quite possible to observe sufficiently on a clear night, especially if you practise at home.

SCOUTING IN AND AROUND VILLAGES.

Generally the precautions detailed above will apply when you are approaching and scouting villages, or any collection of buildings. Back yards, gardens, and enclosures will need careful scrutiny, particularly as to gates and doorways, but you will have to specially study upper stories, their roofs, and windows, and all places likely to hold snipers, churches and towers especially, no matter how ruined.

GOING BY THE STARS.

" Night on the earth poured darkness; on the sea
The wakeful sailor to Orion's star
And Hellicê turned heedful."

Note.—Hellicê is the Great Bear or the Plough—Americans call it the Dipper. Orion is a winter constellation.

"Truth is a fixed star," a very potent comparison. There are millions of stars in the heavens, all ceaselessly moving from east to west. Out of that moving multitude there is only one that is practically stationary, the Pole Star. You can best discover it by the pointers of the Great Bear—or, as it is more appropriately called, the Plough (see B C on Diagram No. 9). Like Truth, it is hard to find sometimes.

The Pole Star is the emblem of Truth, it never varies; further, it is always true north (practically).

The planet Venus, after the moon, is the most brilliant feature in the night sky. It is also a morning and evening star, but it will not guide you safely, nor will even Mars.

Through the Plough (which is the emblem of labour, and, therefore, knowledge) you will find the Pole Star, tiny, but true, and to a Scout greater than all the constellations to be seen at night.

A Scout's knowledge must be compendious indeed to enable him to make accurate use for more than a few minutes of any other star or stars. The Pole Star suffices. Study its position frequently, so that you can spot it quickly; then face it, and extend your left arm towards it, and put the other arm at right angles; it will still point about due east; reverse the order, and you get due west. Behind you, of course, is the south.

There will be times when, though you can detect the pointers in the Plough yet, owing to the clouds, the Pole Star may be invisible; if so, produce the line given by the pointers upwards about five times the distance between them, and you will get roughly the north point.

DIAGRAM No. 9.

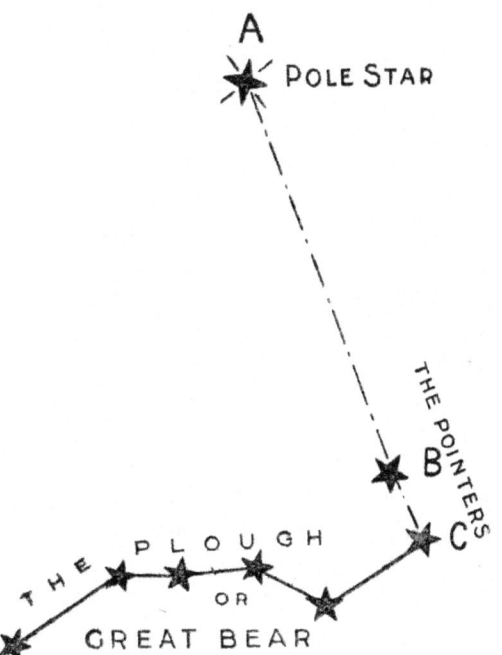

When it is really dark, and there are no stars, then the use of a luminous compass is essential.

USE OF A LUMINOUS COMPASS.

(Refer to Diagram No. 1.)

Lie up in a trench, real or imaginary, in day time, and settle on an objective three or four hundred yards away, and take the exact bearing (say, for example, due south-west) with your compass.

A " Magnapole " compass has two hinged discs, one the real compass, the other a fixed card, marked like the real compass. Over this is a mica covering, on which is a luminous arrow; move the arrow head with your finger and thumb to south-west—the mica can't possibly move afterwards—close the two discs, and your exact bearing is ready at any time.

When it is black dark, put the compass on the ground or in your hand at the place you took the bearing from, and when the north point luminous arrow has steadied down work the luminous dot on the rim of the real compass till it meets the point of the floating arrow. The two will then be in a line with three other dots on the fixed card in the duplicate, all pointing due north, and the arrow on the talc will point to your objective.

If you can see an intermediate object in a line with your objective, noted in the day time, go straight to it, and then use the compass again, and proceed till you arrive at your destination.

Usually there will be no convenient intermediate object, but you can make one by sending a man forward as far as you can see him; signal him to stop, go up to him, extend your line by the compass, and repeat the process, but obviously this will hardly be practical at the Front. You will have to proceed compass in hand, in which case steady your hand with a loop of string round your neck, or crawl, laboriously, and put it on the ground every few yards, following the line south-west.

If you make a zig-zag course for various reasons you won't get where you want to; still, you will always know where the north point is, and sometimes errors equalise themselves.

You will find your way back by following the reverse line shown by the fixed arrow. The compass should be attached to your clothing by stout string.

Laths about 18 inches long, partly treated on one side only with luminous paint, can be made great use of as pointers. These can be seen a fair distance *when you know they are there*, but a casual enemy Scout would hardly notice them. Once the laths have been reached they can be flattened down, and so will be useful on a return journey.

These laths can be used for signalling, and a variety of other purposes.

The presence of rifles in a trench will hardly affect a compass materially unless there are many within a few feet, in which case they are easily removed.

If there are about an equal number of rifles on either side, then the compass will not be affected.

When using a compass put a rifle, if you are carrying one, as far away as you dare; a very few feet will suffice.

It is not necessary to differentiate between true and magnetic north unless you are working to a bearing taken from a map set to true north, in which case you must allow $14\frac{1}{2}°$ west of north for London, $13°$ for Brussels.

Some people consider that there is little need for scouting in trench warfare—that aeroplane work suffices. Two instances alone of clever scouting will show that this view is erroneous.

A British officer at the conclusion of one of my lectures told me the following story :

Four soldiers from his platoon scouted round an enemy observation post in the early hours, and found eight of the enemy fast asleep, and without loss disposed of the lot. This success, most disconcerting to the enemy, was the result of very clever scouting.

According to " The Times," in July last a British officer penetrated through enemy lines a distance of over 1,000 yards, and brought back very important information, which resulted in a great stroke. This officer was indeed a Scout. Try to emulate his wonderful skill, coolness, and courage.

Close Study of Your Surroundings by Day Necessary for Night Work.

(See page 11.)

The vital importance of the above section, written in August, 1915, is dramatically illustrated by the following extract from Sir Ian Hamilton's despatch (Anzac and Suvla), which appeared while the proofs of this lecture were being revised.

Extract from "The Times," 7th January, 1916.

COLUMNS WHICH LOST THEIR WAY.

"At 4.30 a.m. on August 9th the Chunuk Bair ridge and Hill Q were heavily shelled. The naval guns, all the guns on the left flank, and as many as possible from the right flank (whence the enemy's advance could be enfiladed), took part in this cannonade, which rose to its climax at 5.15 a.m., when the whole ridge seemed a mass of flame and smoke, whence huge clouds of dust drifted slowly upwards in strange patterns on to the sky. At 5.16 a.m. this tremendous bombardment was to be switched off on to the flanks and reverse slopes of the heights.

" General Baldwin's column had assembled in the Chailak Dere, and was moving up towards General Johnstone's headquarters. Our plan contemplated the massing of this column immediately behind the trenches held by the New Zealand Infantry Brigade. Thence it was intended to launch the battalions in successive lines, keeping them as much as possible on the high ground. Infinite trouble had been taken to ensure that the narrow track should be kept clear, guides also were provided; but in spite of all precautions the darkness, the rough scrub-covered country, its sheer steepness, so delayed the column that they were unable to take full advantage of the configuration of the ground, and, inclining to the left, did not reach the line of the Farm—Chunuk Bair till 5.15 a.m. In plain English, Baldwin, owing to the darkness and the awful country, lost his way—through no fault of his own. *The mischance was due to the fact that time did not admit of the detailed careful reconnaissance of routes which is so essential where operations are to be carried out by night.*"

The most experienced Scout knows how easy it is to go wrong at night along a stretch of country perfectly familiar by day—the peril is far greater in comparatively strange surroundings, such as "the awful country" mentioned in the despatch.

A recent experience of mine, simple as it was, will make this clear.

Last November I was out, with a keen comrade, late one night studying sounds and the behaviour of horses and cattle in a remote part of Pevensey Marsh, a district I knew intimately. Presently I felt that I had lost my way, for some distance off there appeared, looming up in the moon-lit haze, two huge, unfamiliar objects. Clean done for the moment, I cast round utterly mystified; advancing, I found in the middle of a field a mile away from the nearest road two big farm wagons, piled high with rushes, left for removal another day. No wonder I was misled! This little incident shows how a Scout may get bewildered, for instance, by the unexpected appearance of strange objects. Similar difficulties must occur in a campaign. Shell explosions may remove or alter out of all recognition previously noted landmarks. To pick up a route at night when it is very dark is difficult enough in quiet times and surroundings; it must be tricky work in war, even to the cleverest Scout.

On page 34 there is a short reference to the fact that objects well known by day frequently look totally different by night. It is indeed necessary to " specially study this very awkward phase of night work," particularly in a rough country. A Scout should consider this point when engaged in reconnaissance work by day, and very earnestly, too, which means constant practice at home.

FINIS.

Every Scout in training should go out specially to study all sorts of objects in particular districts by day and their relative positions, and then study them again at night under varying conditions of darkness, the line chosen to be well curved. He should go over the route early next morning and see how and why he got wrong, and also to see by day objects which loomed up large at night and yet were unnoticed in daylight. He will soon get a very fair idea of the difficulties which beset him at every turn; further, he will discover that a luminous compass will give little assistance along a zig-zag route, but he will always know the principal points; this should help if he has taken a few bearings by day.

Paper chases over a limited area would be an interesting way of accustoming men to getting about in the dark, especially in wooded areas.

If feasible, marks should be made at frequent intervals by day, so that the route can be followed on very dark nights, but the best " marks " of all are the twin faculties of intense observation and sense of locality, both the outcome of painstaking labour, without which no Scout can expect to find his way about in the dark.

www.ingramcontent.com/pod-product-compliance
Lightning Source LLC
Chambersburg PA
CBHW060213050426
42446CB00013B/3066